WOHLFAHRT

SIXTY ETUDES
FOR VIOLIN
OPUS 45, *Book 2*

Edited by Eric Wen

LAUREN **K**EISER
MUSIC PUBLISHING

EXPLANATION OF THE SIGNS
ERKLÄRUNG DER ZEICHEN
EXPLICATION DES SIGNES

⊓ | Down bow. *Herunterstrich.* Tirez l'archet.

L. H. | Lower half of the bow. *Untere Hälfte des Bogens.* Moitié inférieure de l'archet.

V | Up bow. *Hinaufstrich.* Poussez l'archet.

T. | Tip (Point) of the bow. *Spitze des Bogens.* A la pointe de l'archet.

W. B. | Whole bow. *Ganzer Bogen.* Employez l'archet en toute sa longueur.

M. | Middle of the bow. *Mitte des Bogens.* Au milieu de l'archet.

U. H. | Upper half of the bow. *Obere Hälfte des Bogens.* Moitié supérieure de l'archet.

N. | Nut of the bow. *Frosch des Bogens.* Au talon de l'archet.

ETUDES

Edited by: Eric Wen

FRANZ WOHLFAHRT
Op. 45, Book 2

№ 31. Moderato

№ 32. Allegro

№ 33. **Allegro moderato**

№ 34. Allegro

№ 35. Allegro

№ 36. Moderato

№ 37. Moderato

10

№ 38. Moderato

№ 39. Moderato
W.B.

№ 40. Allegro scherzando

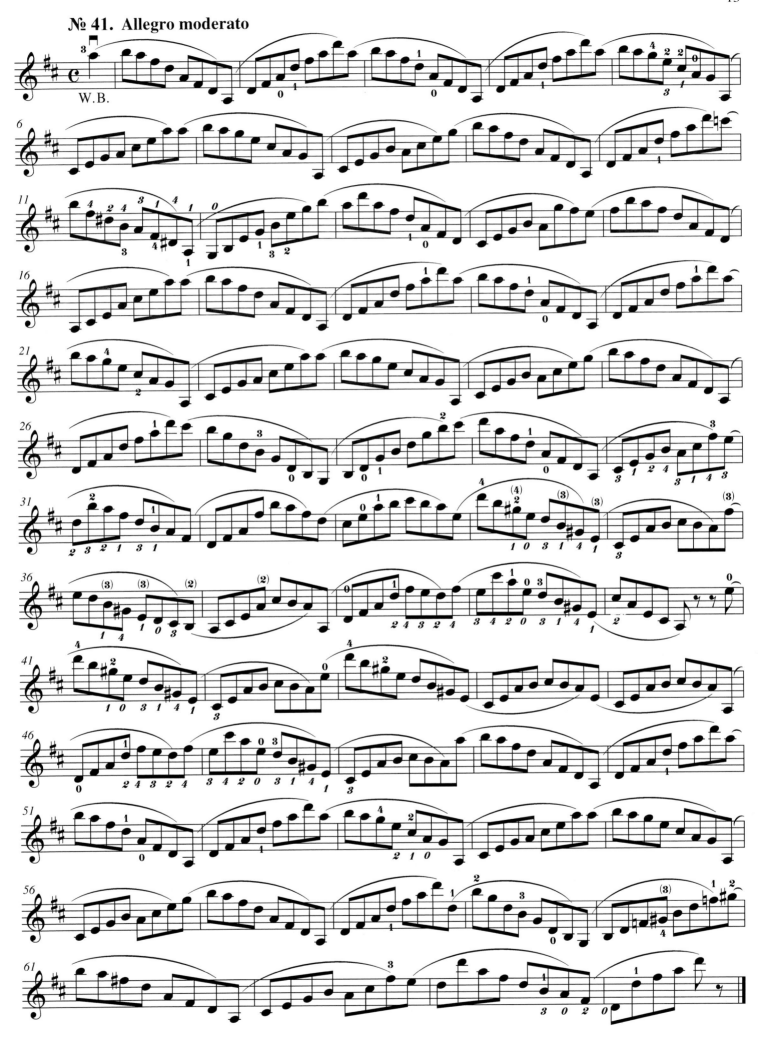

№ 41. Allegro moderato

14

№ 42. Andante

№ 43. Moderato

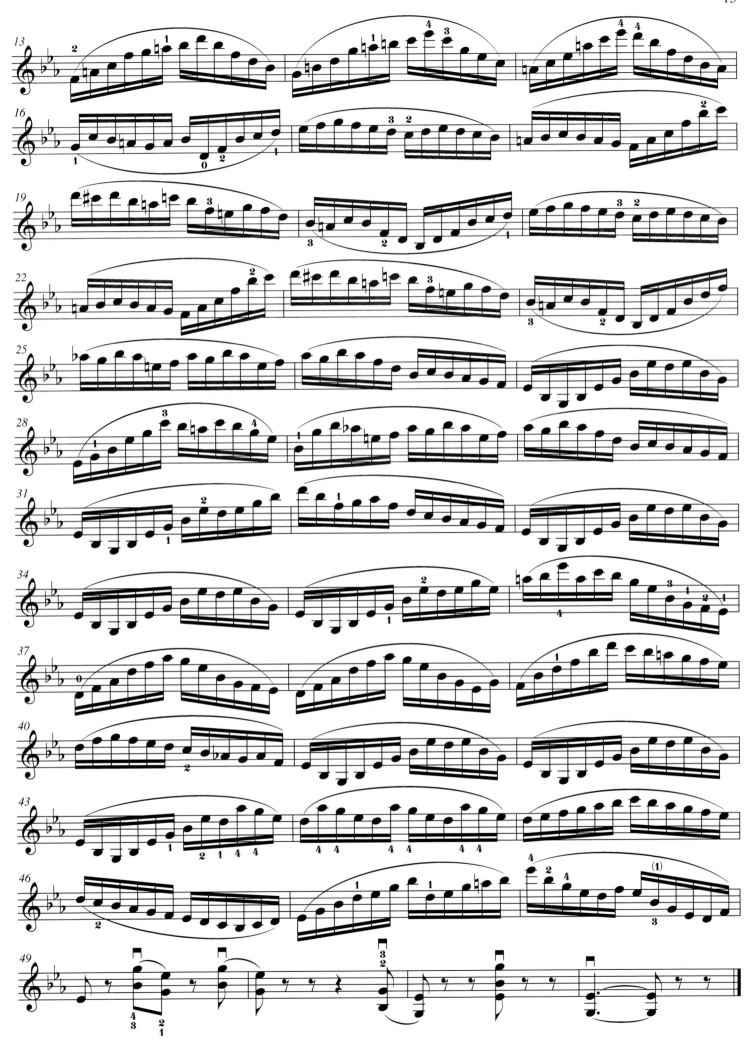

№ 44. Tempo di Marcia

№ 45. Moderato

№ 46. Allegro

№ 47. **Andante cantabile**

22

№ 50. Allegro

№ 51. Moderato

W.B.

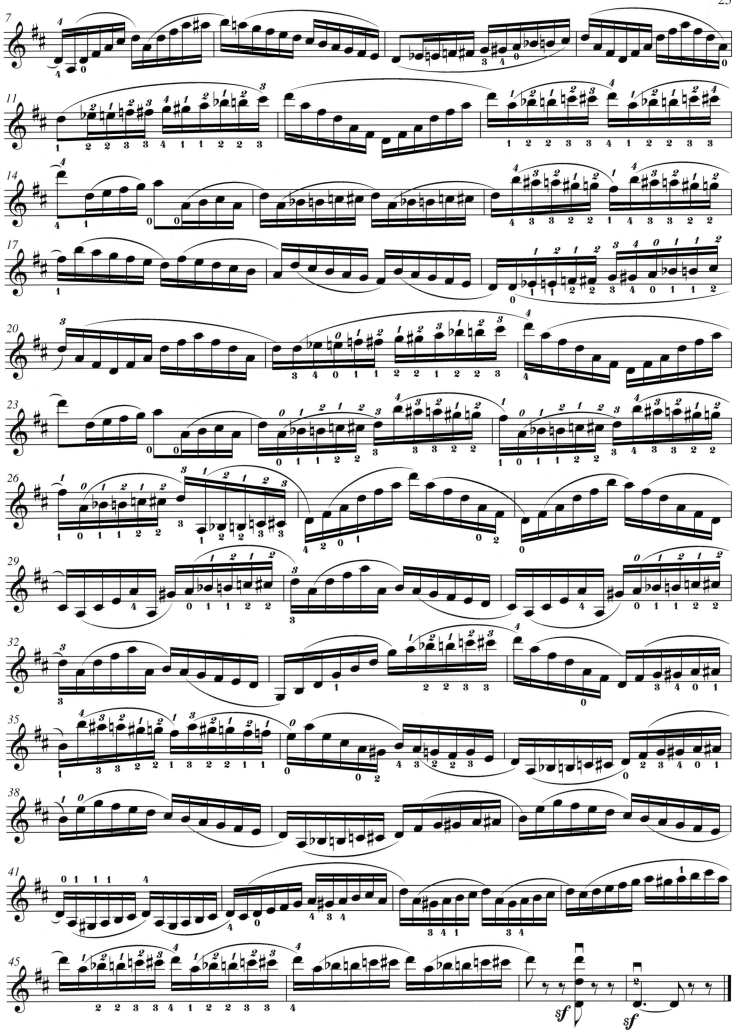

№ 55. Allegro

№ 56. Andante

№ 57. **Moderato assai**

№ 58. **Andante**

№ 59. **Moderato assai**

№ 60. Allegro con fuoco

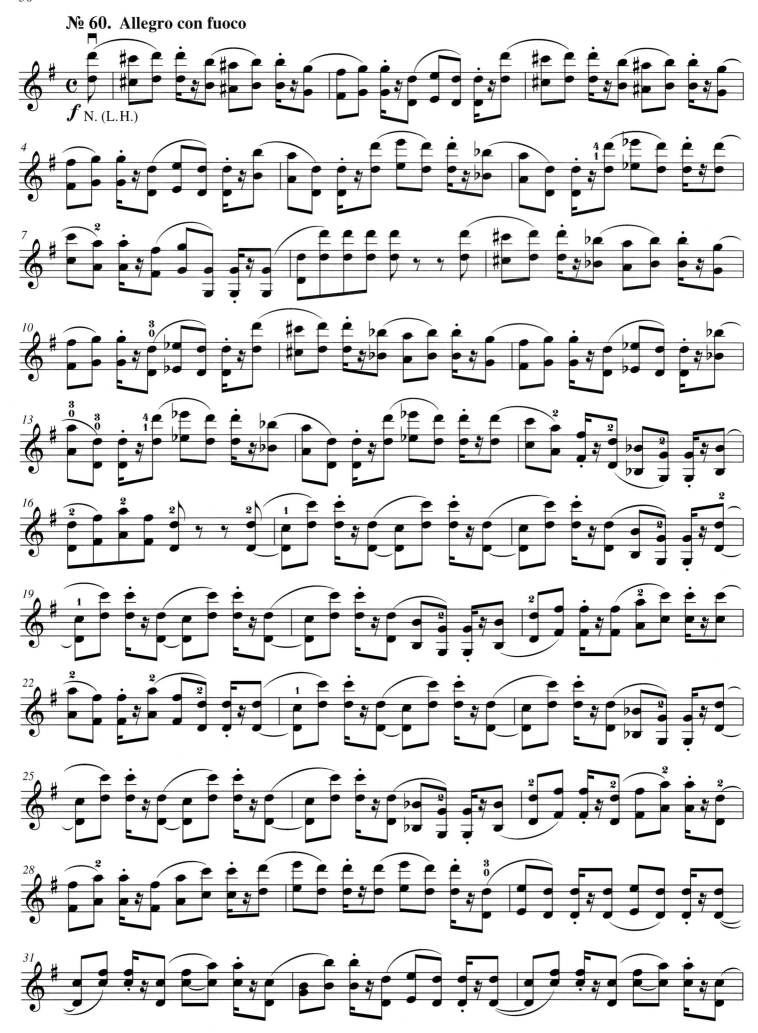

SELECTED VIOLIN SOLO AND CHAMBER MUSIC

Violin

Violin Etudes and Instruction

Wohlfahrt, Franz

S510005 **Sixty Etudes for Violin, Op. 45, Bk. 1**   HL 42303

2011 new issues--former Strad Magazine Editor-in-Chief, Eric Wen re-examines these classics with consideration for today's violinist. All editions newly engraved with handsome color covers and classic 9x12 ivory stock.

ed. Eric Wen

S510006 **Sixty Etudes for Violin, Op. 45, Bk. 2**   HL 42391

Violin Solo, unaccompanied

Adolphe, Bruce

X510011 **Bitter, Sour, Salt Suite**   HL 41866

Can be performed with or without narration, soloist can narrate.

Baker, David

S510001 **Suite for Unaccompanied Violin**   HL 40248

Recorded by Ruggerio Ricci on Laurel Records

Hartke, Stephen

X510012 **Caoine**   HL 41867

Name derived from the laments once sung by the professional wailing women of Ireland; also inspired by the folk fiddling tradition of the Shetland Islands.

Perkinson, Coleridge-Taylor

X510033 **Blue/s Forms**   HL 41886

Three-movement solo violin work fusing blues harmonic language with classical sonata form, recorded by Sanford Allen.

X510032 **Louisiana Blues Strut: A Cakewalk**   HL 41885

Recorded by Sanford Allen on Cedille Records "Coleridge-Taylor Perkinson: A Celebration"

Violin Solo with Keyboard

Baker, David

X511007 **Blues (Deliver My Soul)**   HL 41894

Recorded by Anne Akiko Meyers and Andre Michel-Schub, BMG Records..

S511005 **Ethnic Variations on a Theme of Paganini**   HL 40254

Commissioned By Ruggerio Ricci.

Cooman, Carson

X511035 **Sonata for Violin and Organ**   HL 41918

Crockett, Donald

X511039 **Wet Ink for Violin and Piano**   HL 42418

Violin and piano version of nonet by the same title, dedicated to Steven Stucky for his 60th birthday.

Dancla, Charles

S511010 **Six Airs Varies for Violin and Piano, Op. 89**   HL 42368

2011 new issues--former Strad Magazine Editor-in-Chief, Eric Wen re-examines these classics with consideration for today's violinist. All editions newly engraved with handsome color covers and classic 9x12 ivory stock.

ed. Eric Wen

Sevcik, Otakar

S511012 **Sevcik Op. 16 Wieniawski Scherzo-Tarantelle with Analytical Exercises**   HL 42327

Combines urtext quality solo material with exercises based on renowned 20th-Century violin pedagogue, Otakar Sevcik's, work.

ed. Stephen Shipps

S511014 **Sevcik Op. 17 Wieniawski Concerto Op. 22 in D Minor with Analytical Exercises**   HL TBDS511014

ed. Endre Granat

S511013 **Sevcik Op. 19 Tchaikovsky Concerto Op. 35 in D Major with Analytical Exercises**   HL TBDS511013

ed. Stephen Shipps

S511011 **Sevcik Op. 21 Mendelssohn Violin Concerto in e minor with Analytical Exercises**   HL 42326

ed. Endre Granat

Smith, John Stafford

S511015 **The Star-Spangled Banner (Arranged for Violin and Piano by Jascha Heifetz)**   HL 42616

Along with new engraving for his celebrated transcription, a photo from master violinist Jascha Heifetz's historical collection and a facsimile of the original autograph score adorn this commemorative 9x12 edition.

Stock, David

X511020 **Santa Fe Salsa**   HL 41905

For Andres Cardenes

Walker, George

X511038 **Concerto for Violin and Orchestra (Piano reduction)**   HL 42310

Dedicated to Violinist and Composer Gregory T.S. Walker. Recorded by Gregory Walker, violin and Sinfonia Varsovia, Ian Hobson Conductor, on Albany Records.

Walker, Gwyneth

X511015 **Fantasy Etudes**   HL 41900

Suite of short pieces which can be enjoyed by performers of all ages.

Violin Duo

Hartke, Stephen

X512001 **Oh Them Rats Is Mean in My Kitchen**   HL 41921

Scherzo-fantasy in homage to early blues, transforming its characteristic wailing and energetic speech-song into the seemingly incongruous medium of the violin duo

X512003 **Two Shetland Bridal Tunes**   HL 41923

Two arrangements of traditional Shetland Island fiddle tunes encompassing a processional and recessional, for any festive event or occasion.

Trios, mixed

Violin

Hartke, Stephen

X632711 **The Horse with the Lavender Eye for Violin, Clarinet and Piano**   HL 42074

Four movement tableau of vivid musical images bound together with skillfully crafted 'off-balance' motifs

---

Questions/ comments? Write to: info@laurenkeisermusic.com